Letters To My Dead Parents

Chris J Murphy

Contents

~ { III }

Resources   77

Dedication

Letters To My Dead Parents is a book dedicated to my devoted wife, whose unwavering love and steadfast support have been my anchor throughout the turbulent journey of recovery from addiction, dishonesty, and trauma. Her belief in me has illuminated my path, guiding me toward becoming a better man. I am profoundly grateful for her presence in my life; without her love and encouragement, I would not be the person I am today.

I also want to acknowledge, thank and express my sincere gratitude to the many therapists that I have had the privilege of working with in all my individual, group or intensive therapy sessions during my recovery journey. It is to the therapists in this world that help those in need that we should all honor and respect for their steadfast nature helping others who struggle emotionally through life's traumas.

Author's Note

As I write this, I am a 59-year-old man, navigating the complex and often tumultuous waters of recovery from compulsive and addictive behaviors. These behaviors, which I now recognize as destructive not only to myself but also to those I love, include co-dependency, workaholism, unmanaged alcohol and drug use, overeating, overspending, excessive consumption of media, and, perhaps the most challenging of all, sexual addiction. Each of these patterns has woven itself into the fabric of my life, often serving as a misguided shield against the pain of my past.

The primary focus of this book is to share my story—an account of how a childhood marred by abuse and neglect led me to develop these behaviors as a means of protection and survival. What began as coping mechanisms to navigate a chaotic world gradually morphed into harmful habits that damaged and even destroyed the relationships that I hold dear.

For far too long, I failed to recognize that I was also on the list of those I had harmed. A deep-rooted sense of unworthiness, planted in the fertile soil of my childhood experiences, kept me from loving or even caring for myself. I carried the belief that I was unworthy, unloved, and undeserving into adulthood—a narrative that was never true but felt inescapable. This false story grew into an anxiety disorder, one I denied for years until I finally sought help at the age of 55 and began the journey of healing through therapy and even medication.

This book is not just a recounting of my life; it is a testament to resilience and the possibility of transformation. It is a story that may resonate with your own, filled with hidden secrets, past abuse, regret, and resentment, but also one of joy, love, happiness, and success. I began writing at the suggestion of several therapists who have guided me through the healing process over the past four years. Their unwavering support has enabled me to rebuild myself, and I am now the husband I always aspired to be for my wife. Today, I stand stronger, embracing my true, authentic self—no longer the deceitful, hidden, and selfish man I once was.

If you find yourself grappling with similar struggles—whether they stem from trauma, addiction, or the weight of unprocessed emotions—I hope my story offers you comfort, understanding, and perhaps even a glimmer of hope. You are not alone in your journey. There is a path to healing, and while it may be fraught with challenges, it is also filled with opportunities for growth and connection. Together, we can navigate the complexities of our pasts and emerge into a future where we can embrace our true selves.

Thank you for joining me on this journey. I hope my experiences resonate with you and provide guidance as you navigate your own life's path and recovery.

Chris J. Murphy.
November 11, 2024.

Introduction

This is my third book, yet it is the one I have approached with the deepest reluctance. It's a daunting task for any individual to face their demons, to confront the raw truths that shape their very being. The fear of how these revelations might alter others' perceptions—transforming admiration into disdain, love into rejection—haunts me.

At the heart of my struggle lies an overwhelming fear of abandonment. For much of my life, I navigated through a haze of chaotic emotions, completely unaware of their origins. It wasn't until I began my journey in therapy that the clarity emerged. I had always operated on instinct, driven by an unyielding need to protect myself at all costs, blind to the true price of those defenses. Like countless others, I adhered to societal expectations—I worked hard, sought love, built a family, forged a career, and even landed in a picturesque setting I had long dreamt of. All of this while believing I had fashioned the perfect life. Yet, beneath that carefully curated exterior lay a profound emptiness and fear, cleverly masked by relentless busyness.

This book is a testament to trauma—a recounting of the struggles faced by a young boy navigating the tumultuous landscape of the mid-60s through the early 80s. It was a time when boundaries seemed nonexistent, where adults indulged in self-destructive behaviors without a second thought. Mothers smoked and drank throughout their pregnancies, children were often relegated to the background, and the excesses of sex, alcohol, and drug use permeated the culture. Key parties, designed for swinging couples, felt commonplace; war was not an abstraction but a brutal reality, and big cities loomed as daunting places of fear and uncertainty.

My story is uniquely mine, though threads of it may resonate with others; it might shock some or feel all too familiar to others who might brashly say, "Just get over it; it's in the past." I did that too—suffocated my feelings, bottled them up for nearly my entire life. This coping mechanism nearly cost me everything I had worked tirelessly to build and risked the love of those I held dear. I was unwittingly trekking along a shadowy path, oblivious to the darkness that lay ahead.

Trauma is a deeply individual experience. Throughout my journey, I made it my mission to create a contrasting, nurturing environment for my children, starkly different from the one I had endured. Yet, despite my efforts, they too grapple with their unique traumas—challenges that, seeing them suffer, shatter my heart. I naively believed I could control their world, could shield them from pain. I was wrong. The truth is, all I can do is focus on my own growth, offering them love, acceptance, and respect for their pain and perspectives, while refusing to shoulder the blame for perceived failures in my parenting.

It is my hope, dear reader, that as you journey through these pages, you may begin to unravel the ways your own traumas have shaped you, recognizing those influences that may lie beneath your conscious awareness. In today's world, where isolation often takes precedence, we risk losing the vital human contact essential for our collective well-being and happiness. Thus, we must cultivate the courage to reach out and seek help. We do not have to navigate these storms alone. Each of us has the agency to make different choices; there is an abundance of resources available—from self-care literature to intensive therapy—empowering us to reshape our lives for the better once we acknowledge our truths and accept the dimensions of our lost selves.

My hope is that my story will serve as a beacon of encouragement for you. It may inspire you to confront your own trauma and untangle the pain intertwined with the fractured pieces of your childhood—fragments that, even after all these years, still wield an undeniable influence over your adult responses. Let us embark on this journey together...

Part One - Childhood

Chapter One

Birth to Eight Years - The Early Neglect

I realized early on that I was seen as a burden to my parents—like a stray cat that just wouldn't leave. There exists a blurry line between innocence and burden, and as a child, I waded into that murky water without understanding the depth. One of my earliest memories is of my father regaling other adults with tales of my toddlerhood, where I was apparently a pint-sized tornado wreaking havoc in the living room. He would boast about how I had a knack for running headfirst into every sharp corner of our square glass coffee table, a perilous fixture that became notorious within our family lore. While I don't recall the actual collisions—the way a sudden impact can obliterate memory—I bear the scars on my face as permanent reminders of my clumsiness. The evidence is stark and undeniable, each mark like a chapter etched into my skin.

Even now, as a parent myself, I'm baffled that they didn't think to remove the table after the first incident. Instead, they let me engage in an odyssey of self-destruction with that glass monstrosity, resulting in at least five trips to the ER and a grand total of 50 stitches. Many of those late-night visits etched a familiar routine in my mind—a mixture of fluorescent lights, the smell of antiseptic, and my father's gruff murmurs mingling with my mother's worried silences. It was a cycle that repeated itself, reflecting not only my clumsiness but also a family dynamic steeped in neglect. I suppose I eventually learned to navigate around the table, but by then, the damage was done—both to my face and my sense of safety.

My father embodied a masterclass in selfishness, a man whose insecurities were as palpable as the heavy scent of his scotch that lingered in the air. He prioritized his own needs above those of our family, a king presiding over a crumbling empire. When he did engage in caregiving, it was usually a half-hearted attempt to ease his own guilt—more an obligation than an act of love. Throughout my life, from childhood into my 40s, he found various ways to take advantage of me, often veiled in the guise of paternal affection. Initially, I didn't view him through the same critical lens as my mother, who wielded her discontent like a sword. However, it didn't take long for me to realize that he was not merely flawed but rather a functional alcoholic and a compulsive sex addict—issues that I would have to confront and grapple with over the years. Spoiler alert: it's not a pretty picture.

In those early years, I struggled to fit in, even within the hallowed halls of kindergarten and first grade. I wore the mask of a child trying desperately to blend into the backdrop of normalcy, but the stage felt foreign to me. Yet, amid the struggles, there were moments of joy sprinkled throughout, fleeting instances where laughter echoed in the classroom and hugs from teachers felt warm and genuine. For the first few years of elementary school in upstate New York, I felt safe, cared for, and loved by my teachers. School was my sanctuary, a place where I could pretend to be normal, where the chaos of home miraculously faded away.

But that sense of security was yanked away in the spring of 1972 when my father announced that we would be moving to Florida by the end of summer. Just like that, my life was poised to take a nose-dive into the unknown, an unwelcome turbulence that ignited a million questions in my mind: Why now? What about my friends? Could this new place possibly understand me?

In late August 1972, just after my seventh birthday, we relocated to an isolated island near Sarasota, Florida. Known for its stunning beaches and tropical vibes, it was primarily a retirement haven—a paradise for the elderly but not exactly a bustling playground for kids my age. I found myself struggling to make friends, an awkward social creature amid a sea of gray-haired residents enjoying their golden years. I often longed for companionship, and yet there were only two kids my age living nearby. One of them was a taller-sized bully, who made my life a living hell until I was nine. Spending time with him felt about as appealing as a root canal, and I opted to gradually distance myself from the tumultuous friendship.

Initially, life on the island felt like an adventure, a whimsical escape awash in sunshine and surf. I swam in the hotel pool where my father worked, body surfed at the beach, fished at the harbor across from our house, and rode my bike around the island, feeling the sun on my skin and the wind in my hair. For a brief moment, it was all fun and games—but, as is often the case in my life, the situation at home quickly spiraled into chaos.

My father managed a beachfront hotel that his family had purchased as an investment. It was only half a mile from our home, an easy commute for a man seeking solace through work. But when he returned in the evenings, the air crackled with tension, an electric undercurrent of unspoken frustration. He would pour himself a scotch and water, the clinking of ice echoing like a portent of gloom, as he attempted to engage my mother in conversation. By then, she was usually three sheets to the wind, lost in her own world of inebriation.

After about 20 minutes of futile attempts, he would give up, storming around the room with a cigarette dangling from his lips, exclaiming, "Lilly, talking to you is like talking to a brick wall!" At the tender age of seven, I was already acutely aware of how miserable my father was with my mother.

It wasn't long before my father did what I had dreaded—he decided to leave my mother. I harbored suspicions of his infidelity even before we moved to Florida, but once we settled on the island, he fully embraced a new lifestyle, one that danced dangerously close to recklessness. Surrounded by attractive younger women visiting the island, he frequented bars and indulged in weekly jaunts to the local Lions Club, the thrill of new relationships masking his own insecurities.

Only six months after our move, my father came home one sunny afternoon, radiating a sense of ease that felt foreign in the tense environment. "Chris," he said, his casual demeanor masking the gravity of his words, "I'm leaving your mother. I'm moving into one of the efficiency suites at the hotel. You can visit me anytime, but I want you to stay with her. You're the man of the house now; you need to take care of your mother."

I can't recall exactly how I responded at the time. Part of me was indifferent, thinking it wouldn't be a big deal—children often grapple with detached reasoning. Another part thought, "What a selfish jerk." Simultaneously, a fear began to creep into my heart because I knew how sick my mother was with her alcoholism. I believe that was the moment when I began to crave my father's love, respect, and attention, planting the seeds of my toxic shame—believing I was unworthy, abandoned, and unloved. That shame would follow me throughout my life, lurking in the shadows like a specter, and yet I wouldn't fully grasp its impact until I reached adulthood.

Thus began my journey—a journey shadowed by my father's choices and shaped by an uprooted childhood. Little did I know how these formative experiences would ripple through the fabric of my life, creating waves of pain, confusion, and ultimately, resilience. The echoes of those early years would haunt me, yet they would also challenge me to seek answers, to unravel the tangled threads of my past in hopes of weaving a more hopeful future. It was a hard path ahead, but every step would lead me closer to the truth I desperately needed to uncover within myself.

A Letter to my Dead Parent

Father,

As I sit down to write this letter, I find myself grappling with a whirlwind of emotions—anger, sadness, and a strange sense of longing mingling within me. It's been a decade since you left this world, yet the impact of your choices continues to ripple through my life like a stone cast into a still pond, creating waves I often struggle to navigate. I often wonder if you ever truly understood the weight of your actions and the legacy you left behind, a legacy of pain and disconnection that echoes through every facet of my existence.

From a young age, I felt the burden of your expectations and the shadow of your insecurities looming over me like a dark cloud. You were a man who wore his selfishness like a badge of honor, prioritizing your own needs above our family's. I can still remember those long, tension-filled evenings when you would come home from the hotel, scotch in hand, your frustration palpable as you attempted to engage with a mother who was often lost in her own intoxicated haze. Those moments served as painful reminders of how disconnected we all were, each of us trapped in our own worlds of hurt and disappointment, yearning for connection yet unable to reach one another.

Your decision to leave us was a turning point in my life—one I still grapple with, one that has left scars deeper than any physical wound. When you announced that you were moving into one of the efficiency suites at the hotel, I felt a gut-wrenching mix of confusion and betrayal. You told me I was now the "man of the house," a title I never wanted and was ill-prepared to shoulder at the tender age of seven. How could a child so innocent possibly take on such a weighty responsibility? In that moment, I stopped being just a boy—I was thrust into a role that felt foreign and heavy, the essence of my childhood chipping away under the pressure of expectations that were never rightfully mine to bear.

In the wake of your departure, I was left to navigate a tumultuous sea of emotions without guidance. Confusion morphed into co-dependence, and I became an adult seeking validation and affection from others while desperately trying to fill the vast void you left behind. I sought out people to rescue, convinced that by saving them, I could somehow save myself. As I spiraled through relationships varying in chaos and intensity, I craved the approval and warmth that you never provided. Yet, in my relentless quest for love, I often found myself ensnared in cycles of unhealthy relationships and choices that mirrored your own destructive patterns.

Your absence opened the door to a world of confusion and heartache. It allowed the darkness of childhood sexual abuse to sneak in, a twisted chapter that I now recognize as a horrific reflection of the environment you helped create. The early exposure to adult themes, the chaos of your relationships, and the secrets that festered in our home shaped my understanding of intimacy in deeply unsettling ways. I inherited a pattern of addiction that now feels eerily mirrored in your own struggles—an unending cycle of seeking solace in the very things that ultimately led to our downfall.

I often think about the little boy I once was, the one still crying out for the love, protection, and comfort that were so painfully absent. I wish I could go back in time and tell him that none of it was his fault, that he was worthy *of love, respect, and safety. I wish I could shield him from the pain that would follow, the shame that would cling to him like a second skin, wrapping him in insecurity and heartache for years to come.*

Despite the tempest of anger and hurt that swirls within me, I wrestle with a longing to understand you—a desire that feels both natural and unnerving. I want to believe that beneath the layers of your dysfunction, there resided a man who grappled with his own demons. Perhaps you were molded by the circumstances of your upbringing, a reflection of pain passed through generations. I yearn to forgive you—not for your sake, but for my own healing. Holding onto anger only serves to anchor me to a past I am desperate to break free from. That heaviness is suffocating, and I seek to rise above it.

So, as I write this letter, I am taking a tentative step toward that freedom. I'm acknowledging the pain you caused, but I'm also recognizing the strength I've gained in the process. I am learning to let go of the burdens you left behind, to release the little boy still searching for your approval. It's a complex dance of grief and healing, and I'm determined to find my rhythm within it.

Wherever you are, I hope you can finally grasp the profound impact of your choices. I hope you can see the man I have become—a mosaic shaped by both the darkness and the light of my experiences. With every letter I write, each word becomes a testament to my journey toward healing, a step toward rebuilding the fragmented pieces of my soul.

With a heart that seeks peace,
Your Adult Son,
Chris

{ 2 }

Chapter Two

E ight to Fourteen Years - The Sexual Abuse

The years between the ages of eight and fourteen marked a turbulent period in my life, establishing the groundwork for one of my most crippling compulsions: sex addiction. I find it cruelly ironic that my mother, ensnared in her own battle with sex addiction, unintentionally bequeathed this painful legacy to me. At just seven years old, I was blissfully ignorant of these destructive patterns, merely a confused, vulnerable boy trying to navigate a chaotic world that felt perpetually on the verge of collapse.

During those formative years, I bore witness to harrowing scenes that would later haunt my adult life. With a mix of horror and disbelief, I watched my mother, intoxicated and adrift in her loneliness, engage in impassioned make-out sessions with a parade of men on our dilapidated couch. Their drunken laughter reverberated throughout our home, intertwining with the unmistakable sounds of intimacy—moans and gasps filtering through the slatted doors of her bedroom, which offered no real sanctuary from the staggering reality just out of sight. I was but an unwilling spectator in a twisted play where love had devolved into something sordid and terrifying.

When my father designated me the "man of the house," instructing me to care for her, I internalized that burden. How else could I earn his love and attention? As a bewildered child, I craved not only approval but affection that seemed perpetually elusive. While my mother sought companionship in the arms of anyone willing to offer a fleeting glance, I grappled with the weighty expectation of being her emotional anchor.

Of all the faces that drifted in and out of my mother's life, one man stands out starkly—a figure who would later sexually abuse me at the age of eleven. Just the thought of him sends waves of visceral fear coursing through me, leaving me numb and nauseated. His presence epitomized the tragic fallout of a home devoid of safety and stability, and that traumatic experience proved a pivotal moment in my young life.

What I lay bare in this chapter fills me with deep shame, even now. I engaged in behaviors that I instinctively knew were wrong, yet somehow rationalized them as acceptable because my mother had normalized such actions. I remember the stirrings of sexual arousal as early as eight years old—a far too complex and frightening experience for a child raised in an environment stripped of healthy boundaries and adult guidance. With my mother's behavior serving as a warped template, I was left to navigate my feelings in isolation. The actions taken during this period planted the seeds of profound shame within me—a gnarled root that would require years of therapy to unravel. I can only speculate about the memories I've buried deep within my consciousness, yet specific incidents remain etched in my mind, leading me down a shadowy path of inappropriate sexual fantasies, deceit, and secrecy in my adult relationships.

After my father moved out, my exploration of my mother's hidden world commenced when I stumbled upon magazines tucked away under her bed. What I discovered shocked me—two distinct types of magazines that deeply unsettled my young mind. One showcased explicit pornography featuring men and women, while the other displayed scenes of bestiality, depicting a blonde woman and a male horse. Reflecting on this later, it became abundantly clear that my mother was drawn to exceptionally disturbing content—an unsettling revelation that only deepened my confusion. I never broached the topic with her; I remained too bewildered and, in a twisted way, intrigued. After all, my mother was overtly sexual in our home, often parading around in her underwear and using the bathroom in full view while I took my baths. To her, these behaviors felt completely normal; to me, they felt profoundly wrong.

Not long after, my mother's sisters began to visit from Sweden for month-long stays. I was around eight years old then, and they were vibrant, attractive women in their late twenties—carefree and spirited. They sunbathed by our pool, unabashedly topless, flaunting their bodies without a hint of self-consciousness, a stark contrast to the confused child trying desperately to grasp what was appropriate and what was not. They entered the bathroom while I bathed, giving me fleeting glimpses of their bare bodies, which ignited an obsession within me—an overwhelming fixation on women's breasts and nipples. It was during this time that I experienced my first erections, often accompanied by dreams featuring my aunts—dreams that left me exhilarated yet profoundly bewildered.

I remember asking my mother why one of her sisters, who had brought her son along, didn't bring her husband and why they felt so comfortable being naked. She explained that, in Sweden, it was perfectly normal for mothers to have children without fathers, and that going topless was as natural for women as it was for boys to swim without shirts. Her words, though intended to reassure, only deepened the confusion and damage within me. I internalized her explanations, mistakenly believing that this was how the world operated—an understanding so misguided it would take years to untangle. The web of misconceptions and shame she unknowingly wove around me would shape my views on intimacy and self-worth, ensnaring me in a cycle of confusion that would persist well into my adulthood.

As I transitioned from nine to ten years old, my attraction and sexual desires intensified. I entered into puberty early, likely a consequence of the relentless exposure to sexual situations I had witnessed over the past three years with my mother and her ever-changing parade of companions. During this time, a younger man in his late twenties named Weston began living with us. He was always kind to me, which left little room for complaint, especially since he sometimes made an effort to keep my mother sober. Yet, there lingered a sense of discomfort—he was sleeping with her, and it just felt wrong.

One weekend, we ventured to a bar on the mainland where a cute blonde girl befriended my mother and Weston. My mother agreed she could stay with us, resulting in her taking my bed while I was relegated to the couch. That shift spoke volumes about my role in the family and filled me with bitterness. Yet, I couldn't deny my attraction to this girl, who claimed to be eighteen. She stayed with us for about three weeks and one night, while we swam in the pool, she kissed me—not a quick peck, but a deep, lingering French kiss that lasted two exhilarating minutes. It felt incredible. The experience was a vivid manifestation of the juxtaposition between my innocence and the burgeoning older woman's interest in me. Nothing more transpired between us, but I remembered that moment distinctly. The knowledge that she was clearly sexual, often retreating to my mother's bedroom with Weston, heightened my burgeoning interest in older women and distorted my understanding of mutual attraction.

Toward the end of her stay, the police eventually discovered her whereabouts and took her away—she was, in fact, a fourteen-year-old runaway. I was left puzzled as to why she had kissed me so passionately until I learned her true age, which brought clarity, but also a lingering fantasy that older women might reciprocate my interest—a notion that would soon haunt me. I don't recall discussing her with my mother after she left, nor do I remember her name. Yet, that first kiss remains engraved in my memory, profoundly impacting my young mind.

My mother had a close friend named Daisy, a somewhat severe but functional alcoholic who spent considerable time with us. Daisy owned a hair studio on the island and lived above her shop. During my nine and ten-year-old years, my mom and I often frequented Daisy's apartment. Daisy was kind to me, comforting me by rubbing my back and tucking me in at night when my mother slipped into drunkenness in the next room. Yet, during those encounters, I found myself developing an attraction toward Daisy, urging her to engage in inappropriate touching, which she firmly rebuffed. Regardless, I harbored intense fantasies about her—a secret longing that would shadow me for much of my life.

Daisy had a boyfriend named Walter, a musician who worked at a local German restaurant. He was a clown, frequently joking and often drunk, but he never made me feel unsafe. One Friday night at Daisy's apartment, the three of them—my mother, Daisy, and Walter—overindulged and eventually passed out on the king-sized bed while I slept on the couch. Around 2 AM, I awoke to the sensation of a mouth enveloping me, stirring me from slumber. My initial thought was that Daisy was acting on my previous advances. But when I peeked, I was horrified to find it was Walter instead. In a desperate attempt to protect myself, I feigned sleep. I cannot explain why I didn't scream at that moment; I realized later that I had previously endured a traumatic incident at eight years old with a neighbor and his father who lured me into their shed asking me to "Play with Him". When I was able to escape and told my mother, she was reprimanded by the neighbor and his wife and told me to forget about it and perhaps it did not happen in order to keep peace in the neighborhood.

From that event, I avoided any further trauma at this time, so I let it happen. The following day, Walter drove me home, casually asking if I remembered anything. I lied, saying no, and as he grinned, I felt a chill sweep over me—I could sense he felt he had escaped scot-free. This event would haunt my sexuality for the rest of my life, filling me with shame and propelling my burgeoning sex addiction and attraction to women further. For decades, I kept this secret buried deep, unaware of the profound impact it would have on my future relationships and my marriage.

Three months after that incident, one of my father's old girlfriends named Darla visited my mother. Darla had been with my father for about two years when I was eight and nine. I remembered well how I had knocked on my dad's efficiency apartment door one afternoon only to hear them rush to dress in a frantic attempt to conceal that I had interrupted their intimate time. Darla had parted ways with my father upon his meeting a younger woman named Kate, who would eventually become my stepmother. Darla's return to our lives was driven by the desire to present my mother with a picture of a daughter she claimed was fathered by my dad during their relationship. While my mother may have felt confused and angry, caught in the web of her own struggles, she also sympathized—a fellow woman confronted by the same deadbeat man she had married. I was genuinely excited about the prospect of having a sister, yet this meeting would not happen until I took the initiative to do so at the age of twenty-seven.

In a reactive move, my father decided that my mother and I needed to leave the house, unable to maintain the bills. In truth, he yearned to move in with Kate, who was twenty-two when they met, in a house he had previously shared with my mother. So, my mother and I relocated to an apartment on the mainland while my father and Kate settled into our former home to renovate it for sale.

No longer burdened by Walter's presence, I resumed my role as my mother's caretaker, now witnessing her further decline into alcoholism and loneliness. Her isolation deepened, and she spent her days drinking and chatting on the phone with friends, while I struggled to forge new friendships, leading me down the path of early drug use. My new friends, a brother and sister recently moved from Miami to Sarasota, introduced me to the thrill of getting stoned on a daily basis.

As I rebelled against my mother by gaining freedom with my 10-speed bike, I found adventure with my new friends—buying Marlboro cigarettes from K-Mart vending machines and wandering the neighborhood in various antics. My mother's loneliness intensified, and although my anger toward her grew, a part of me still felt an obligation to care for her.

By the time I turned twelve, I was knee-deep in my rebellion—an unrepentant pothead, neglecting my own care, all while she sunk deeper into her alcohol-induced stupor. Each night, I fell asleep with Pink Floyd's "The Dark Side of the Moon" spinning on my Koss headphones, embraced by the music. Then, one weeknight, my mother entered my room topless and in her underwear, climbing into my single bed beside me. It was clear to me what she was seeking; she was heavily intoxicated and likely just wanted to be held. Yet, I instinctively reacted by getting out of bed and demanding she leave my room. The scene endures in my memory, 47 years later—a moment of ultimate rejection for her. This rejection mirrored the night Walter abused me, resonating in a way that struck deep within my psyche. I feared what would transpire if I permitted her to stay—afraid my own sexual boundaries might crumble, leading to even more traumatic experiences.

That night marked a grim turning point, and I cannot help but feel responsible for the subsequent six months of turmoil. Afterward, I ceased speaking to her about that night; perhaps she forgot, but I certainly didn't. Such events would lay the groundwork for the anxiety that would follow me into adulthood, although I would stubbornly refuse to acknowledge my struggles with anxiety until I turned fifty-eight.

With my mother perpetually inebriated, I organized a party for my pothead friends at our house. Every other weekend, I stayed with my father and my new stepmother on the Island, sharing a room with my stepbrother who was eight years younger. I despised being there, feeling stifled without the freedom I enjoyed on the mainland with my mother. For my thirteenth birthday, which fell on a Saturday that year, I eagerly anticipated having about seven friends over to celebrate. My mother remained drunk downstairs, blissfully unaware of the chaos unfolding upstairs.

We rolled six joints, igniting all at once, passing them around as we cranked up various albums on the turntable. Some friends brought beer; they drank, while I stuck to the high of marijuana.

Before my thirteenth birthday, an old friend of my mother, visiting from New York State, informed me that upon turning thirteen,

I could express to the courts my desire to stay with my mother, and they would honor my request. During this time, my father sought full custody of me, aiming to keep me away from my mother's volatile environment. Yet, the judge displayed sympathy towards my mother's plight. I didn't want to leave her. I had grown fond of her, despite her flaws, and I felt a strong desire to protect her. The news from my mother's friend encouraged me—I could advocate for my mother and refuse to move in with my father. Unfortunately, that plan unraveled spectacularly.

After the party on Sunday, I called my father to inform him that I wouldn't return to live with him—my newfound knowledge emboldened me. My mother was thrilled to hear my declaration, yearning for our bond even though it was severely unhealthy. But my father was furious, shouting that he would come for me. I stood my ground, unwilling to budge. Later that evening, he and two police officers came to our house, dragging me out and causing a disgraceful scene for my mother and me alike. It was a dark, dreadful night.

Weeks later, my father secured full custody in court, citing the events surrounding my raucous birthday party as evidence of inadequate supervision, with witnesses testifying to the drinking and drug use occurring in our home. From that point on, I could only visit my mother every other weekend.

Believing I needed reform, my father and Kate enrolled me in a Christian school that August. I faced the humiliation of cutting my long hair, conforming to rigid standards—standing when adults entered the room and wearing a uniform—a stark departure from my previous life. This marked the first shift toward a desk-bound existence consumed by an addiction to God or religion, which would take root during my eighth to tenth grades. I resented this change, harboring animosity toward Kate, yet I couldn't shake my attraction to her, given that she was just ten years older than me.

During this time, we moved off the Island into a rental house in Manatee county. I was now forced to attend public school again, as the distance to the Christian School was considerable. At least I could begin to grow my hair again, but I weathered the storm of adjustment, feeling increasingly disoriented in my new reality. The weekends spent with my mother blended into a haze; her condition continually worsened. I barely recall the last time I saw her or spoke to her—it may have been Christmas of 1978, but the memory escapes me.

On Saturday, January 6th, my father delivered the news: my mother was in a coma in the hospital after falling and hitting her head. I begged to see her, but he would not permit it. The following day, Kate informed me of her passing. I felt numb—the world blurred around me as I grappled with confusion. A haunting anxiety loomed over me; I had always worried about the possibility of her death. I began internalizing blame, questioning my role in propelling her toward an inevitable demise—an unshakable burden that left me lonely and alien from my peers, as I navigated the treacherous waters of the eighth grade.

In retrospect, those years didn't unfold as mere chaos; they represented a pivotal chapter in my life—one marked by an unrelenting quest for affection in all the wrong places. The pain, confusion, and burgeoning shame intertwined to craft a tapestry that would take years of healing to unravel. As I progressed into adolescence, the scars of those formative experiences would accompany me, unwelcome yet inescapable, as I sought connection in a fragmented world.

A Letter to my Dead Parent

Mother,

As I stand on the threshold of retirement, I find myself drawn into the depths of my past—a tumultuous sea of memories that remind me, unrelentingly, of the shadow you and Father cast over my childhood. It is not an easy task, nor a comfortable one, to confront the tangled web of emotions you left in your wake. Yet, it is a journey I must undertake, as these unresolved feelings cling to me, each a flickering candle in the dark, yearning for the light of understanding.

Your neglect during my formative years imparted a cruel lesson about trust—a delicate treasure easily shattered. In my need to shield myself from the hurt, I became a skilled liar, weaving a veil of deceit that ensnared not just me, but those I held most dear—especially my beloved wife. In my misguided efforts to protect myself, I ended up betraying the one person who deserved my truth, my openness, and my love.

When I cast my mind back to that innocent child I once was, I am overwhelmed with a potent surge of anger and sorrow. He was forced to navigate a treacherous landscape of neglect and emotional turmoil, all while bearing the unsettling burden of an exposure to adult sexuality that no child should ever endure. This painful environment molded him into a guarded, secretive version of himself—one who became trapped in a cycle of seeking validation and approval from friends and authority figures, all while grappling with a sense of unworthiness that weighed heavily on his heart.

The shadows of the sexual abuse I endured from ages seven to twelve have left scars that run far deeper than skin. They carved pathways in my psyche, shaping me into a man caught in the grips of addiction—a legacy I now recognize as intertwined with both you and Father. The early encounters with pornographic images, your openly casual relationships, and the disorienting sight of my aunts wandering about so carefree—all of this planted seeds of confusion and distortion in my young mind. Instead of a childhood nourished by innocence and love, I grew ever more entangled in a web of inappropriate attractions and shame—dark secrets that flourished in silence and shadow. When this hidden turmoil was finally brought to light in my marriage, it shattered the trust I had sworn to protect, leaving a deep and painful chasm between my wife and me.

I know I made choices that tangled my life further, yet I cannot ignore the profound impact of the secrecy and mistrust rooted in my early experiences. I locked my pain and confusion away in the darkest corners of my mind, too frightened to seek help and too embarrassed to speak of it.

Even after all these years, your absence lingers, palpably suffocating and unyielding. Writing to you at the end of this chapter serves as an essential practice for my healing—a courageous act of liberation. I now see that clinging to this burden has kept me bound to you, a love-hate tether that is both painful and familiar. That little boy within me still cries out for the love, safety, and affection he never received. I find myself revisiting him in my heart, striving to rescue him from the anguishing sufferings of our past, yearning to offer him the solace that always eluded him.

Wherever you may be, I hope you can finally grasp the magnitude of the pain that resonates within me. It is only through this understanding that I may begin to heal and untangle my heart from your grasp. I commit to continuing these letters, sharing my story—each word a sacred step toward liberation, a fragment of my journey to embrace peace.

With a heart heavy yet hopeful, and a spirit striving for serenity,
Your Adult Son,
Chris

Chapter Three

F ourteen to Eighteen Years - The Search for Survival

The next four years of my life could easily be described as a storm—relentless and unyielding—each wave crashing harder than the last. I was still grappling with the aftermath of my mother's death, a profound loss that had hollowed me out, and now I found myself thrust into a home I never wanted to be in. The upheaval of my world only spiraled deeper as my father, feeling an inexplicable urgency to reclaim normalcy, decided it was best for me to return to a Christian school. He and Kate assured me that this new institution wouldn't be as strict as the previous one we had attended. However, this new Dutch Reformed Christian school felt like an alien landscape—a place where acceptance seemed to hinge upon one's lineage. If you weren't Dutch Reformed by birth, you were an outsider. And here I was, entering my freshman year of high school, cloaked yet again in the rags of solitude and rejection. My history, my struggles—none of that mattered to my peers. To them, I was merely the stranger in the corner, a puzzle piece from a different box.

Despite the frosty reception from my classmates, I felt an instinctual pull to try and fit in. I embraced the idea of "embracing the suck," a philosophy I would later hear echoed in the work world by colleagues. I plunged into my new life, buoyed by the hope that perhaps this time I could forge connections. Kate was relentless in her endeavors to involve me in church activities; I found myself attending services twice a week and participating in youth group meetings. Despite being counted among the band as a flutist—ironically, assigned last chair—I relished the moments spent creating music, the beauty of the notes becoming a temporary escape from the storms brewing in my heart. Ironically, typing class began to stand out as the sole academic experience that imparted a tangible skill, a lifeline I could grasp firmly as I maneuvered the turbulent waters of adolescence.

Yet at the heart of this chaotic existence was Kate's tough love. Ever since that single moment during my first week living under her roof when I had lashed out and told her to "fuck off," my father had made it unmistakably clear: if I ever upset her again, I would be sent to drug rehab. The weight of that threat, ominous as it was, kept my mouth shut and my emotions shrouded. It wasn't long before I mastered the art of suppressing my feelings, burying the pain so deeply that it became a second language.

Diving deeper into the complex labyrinth of my mind, my relationship with Kate grew increasingly convoluted. On one hand, I harbored an inexplicable, sincere affection for her, a remnant of childhood innocence that intertwined itself with something darker—an anger festering within me that couldn't be soothed. I would find myself watching her sunbathe from the confines of my room, grappling with feelings of an unwelcome attraction that took me by surprise. Like a moth drawn to a flame, I was simultaneously tempted and repelled by her presence. It was like being trapped in a twisted version of an Aesop fable; I was entranced, yet feared the burn.

Unbeknownst to her, during those years, I stumbled upon what could only be described as a Pandora's box—Penthouse magazines and 38MM pornographic films hidden away in their bedroom. It was a discovery both enthralling and horrifying. The images sparked a toxic fuel that ignited my imagination, tying together the innocent fantasies of youth with the carnal desires I struggled to acknowledge. I instinctively believed these artifacts belonged more to her than my father and indulged myself in a surreal world of self-created obsessions that echoed my earlier fantasies about Daisy. However the reality was that the pornography really belonged to my Father who was the one addicted to sex and pornography and I was unable to face that truth then, since it was more exciting for me as a teenage boy to stick with the fantasy about Kate

And so, I drifted farther into the web of contradiction. While I outwardly embraced my identity as a good Christian boy, nourished by the rigid teachings of my school, internally I was embracing a hidden life of dark fantasies. At fourteen, I found myself devoid of genuine romantic relationships, yet like any other boy my age, the urgent call of puberty manifested itself, leading me into compulsive acts of masturbation. The unrelenting hush of Kate's bedroom became my illicit haven, where the porn I would sneak a peek at became an insidious dopamine reward—a quick thrill amidst the drudgery of daily life. Those sanctified, early exposures to erotic imagery became foundational moments, planting seeds for a future entanglement with my addiction to pornography when technology would eventually offer me more outlets.

The war within me raged on. I felt like a split personality; on one hand was a boy who yearned to be good, to embody the virtues planted in me from my Christian upbringing—a belief in a loving God. Yet, the institutions of faith, as I knew them, painted a terrifying picture of an unforgiving deity who condemned anyone not saved and baptized. Steeped in this religious fervor, I sought refuge, and as my fifteenth birthday approached, I decided to heed the request of my church leaders, trawling my way to the front of the congregation and agreeing to be baptized—a clear display of devotion in a chaotic life.

But then, a fanaticism began to take root. I let go of my treasured rock albums, convinced that they were vessels of evil corrupting my soul. Beneath this misplaced strength lay an undercurrent of resentment—angst towards my father and Kate mutated into something darker. I rationalized my disdain, fueled by the righteousness instilled in me by church doctrine, believing them both sinners unworthy of grace. They had wronged me, the memory of my mother left in tatters, and I clung to my spiritual fervor as a misguided shield against the pain they had caused.

It wasn't until a defining moment during a summer camp music trip between my sophomore and junior years that the dissonance of my life hit me like a freight train. The camp was fervently focused on a production intended for a thousand churchgoers—a venture that quickly morphed into a drudgery of endless rehearsals, forced labor, and a shocking absence of joy. Under the fervent control of a fanatical preacher, we were subjected to ten-hour days. It felt less like an artistic endeavor and more like a cult experiment, stripping us of individuality, agency, and the very essence of fun. I was not merely exhausted; I was enraged, yearning for autonomy and space. But escape was an illusion; I was trapped in this relentless cycle.

Returning home from the camp, a revelation washed over me. I sat down with my father and Kate, pouring out my heart, explaining how I felt chained to my rigid beliefs, caught up in an addiction to religion that warped my mindset. It was a painful, raw admission, a definitive apology for my turbulent behavior. They suggested I should return to public school for the remainder of high school. A burden lifted; the relief washed over me, akin to shaking the shackles of an oppressive confinement.

At fifteen, I took my first job, stepping into the dynamic milieu of a restaurant—a world that would lead me down the path I would eventually pursue. My tenure began with a regular burger joint, the work awkward and menial. Yet, it soon transitioned into a position at a local retirement home where I honed my skills as a pot washer and dishwasher. This place had a rhythm that resonated with me; my responsibilities expanded to serving thousands of meals daily, a crucial component in the lives of those who resided there.

For the first time in my life, I felt a true sense of belonging, respect, and affirmation. This role grounded me as a fledgling adult, and in the sweltering kitchens, where camaraderie ran high and laughter replaced the loneliness I'd known, I thrived. The fulfillment I garnered propelled me toward culinary school, a vision of my future that filled me with excitement. I could see possibilities unfolding, paths leading to a rewarding career that felt brighter than anything I had previously envisioned.

Paradoxically, while I was exhilarated by my newfound profession, my family life was a different story altogether. My father's long-dormant sorrow erupted when he lost his job during my junior year. He succumbed to an overwhelming depression and took to taking up residence on the couch, enveloped in the comfortable embrace of doubt and despair. Meanwhile, Kate and I became the unlikely breadwinners, our financial contributions barely managing to keep our household afloat. This asymmetry bred resentment within me; I felt the weight of expectations thrust upon my shoulders. My father, who once was my supposed rock, seemed content to deflect any responsibility.

Through it all, I clung fiercely to my culinary aspirations. I was determined that I would not follow in his footsteps, setting my sights on maintaining stability and success. The acceptance letter from Culinary School in Rhode Island—my golden ticket to new beginnings—arrived like a burst of sunlight through dark clouds.

The early days in this newfound vocation ignited something within me. I became a workaholic not just by necessity, but also as an escape from my chaotic familial interactions. I logged hours at my job, not merely for monetary gain, but rather for the affirmation—employing the culinary world as a refuge to mask, and ultimately bury, the pain that still clawed at my insides. I was determined to bypass the disquiet of my home life by immersing myself in the heat of the kitchen.

As I navigated through my last year of high school and anticipated moving north, I felt a profound sense of hope. The thought of being away from Kate and my father ignited a sense of joy within me. No more constraints, no one telling me what was right or wrong. This liberation, this long-desired autonomy was tantalizingly close.

Romantic entanglements remained a challenge, as I wrestled with the strain of living a double life. I dated a sweet girl two years younger than me, treating her with the respect she deserved, yet secretly harboring unsettling fantasies that danced like ghosts in the back of my mind—far from the norms of my emerging sense of self. I wore masks gracefully, presenting an affable exterior while wrestling with the torment of my hidden thoughts. The trauma of my past intertwined with toxic shame, shackled beneath layers of pleasing façades I had carefully constructed.

Finally, on the cusp of turning 18 in July—a month from my departure to college—I felt exhilarated like a bird about to take its first flight. Hope was the wind beneath my wings. This new chapter promised freedom and possibilities, and for the first time in a long while, I could see a bright, different future awaiting me. Isolated beneath daunting waves for so long, I was finally poised to break away, just out of reach from the clutches of my past, seeking my own path, guided only by the desires that flourished within—a life built on my own terms.

A Letter to my Dead Parent

Father,

As I sit down to write this letter, I'm enveloped by a bittersweet tide of emotions—sadness, frustration, and a lingering sense of what could have been. I can't help but reflect on the years we shared, especially during my adolescence, a time marked by transition and turmoil, which, in many ways, shaped who I am today. There's so much I wish I could have shared with you during those years and so much I still carry that feels stuck between us, like a stain on a cherished memory.

Your absence, both physical and emotional, has left echoes in my life that resonate deeply. I often wonder: why did you choose to retreat into the shadows when I needed you most? I look back at the time when you lost your job and went through a deep depression, resigning yourself to a life of watching television instead of actively participating in our family's struggles. Did you realize that your inaction cast a long shadow over my formative years? I felt like I was standing at a precipice, teetering on the edge, desperate for guidance yet left to fend for myself.

There were countless moments when I needed your support, not merely as a father providing for his family but as a role model showing me what it means to face challenges. Instead, I saw a man paralyzed by despair, and while I understand now that you were grappling with your own battles, I also experienced the heavy burden of feeling abandoned. Your choice to remain passive impacted me profoundly. I had to step into the role of caretaker for both you and Kate while still navigating my own turbulence—a weight that often felt unbearable for a teenager.

When I took on those early jobs, it wasn't just about earning a paycheck. It was my way of embracing responsibility, of carving out a sense of belonging in a world that often felt chaotic. I poured myself into those roles, yearning for approval and validation. I wanted to make you proud, to show you that hard work could yield results—but I also hoped you would notice my efforts and perhaps join me in tackling our collective challenges. Instead, I found myself working harder so we could keep our heads above water, while you seemed content to sit idly by.

As I continued to push through high school and embark on early adulthood, I consistently felt torn between admiration for your potential and resentment for your decisions. I grappled with anger for the years I perceived as lost—years that you could have used to inspire me, to teach me the value of resilience and hard work. Instead, I was left to navigate my struggles alone, steeling myself against a world that seemed cold and indifferent.

In my journey toward finding my place, I continually wished for more encouragement from you, less judgment and more understanding. I longed for moments when you would validate my hopes and dreams, celebrate my victories, or even guide me when I faltered. Yet there were no such moments; instead, I was often met with silence or an inability to engage because the weight of your despair was too heavy for either of us to lift.

Looking back, I recognize that your struggles were undoubtedly tied to the wounds of your own past, trials that I may never fully understand. I only wish you could have shared them with me, that you could have trusted me to stand by your side as you faced adversity. Perhaps together, we could have created a space for healing—not only for you, but for me as well.

As I've navigated adulthood, I've come to terms with these feelings that initially felt like chains binding me to resentment. Yet, as I write this letter, I find myself teetering on the precipice of forgiveness, attempting to replace the sadness with understanding. Your absence has taught me a valuable lesson about responsibility and resilience, even if it came wrapped in layers of pain.

I write with the hope of healing—not just for myself, but also for the memory of the man I wished you could have been during those critical years. I'm learning to acknowledge that while your choices left me feeling abandoned, they've also fueled my drive to become a better man, a father, and a role model for those around me. Your legacy will forever be a part of my journey, one that I'm determined to shift from sadness to strength.

Wherever you may be now, I hope you can understand the depth of my feelings, not just the sorrow but also the longing for connection that was never fully realized. This is my way of letting go, my attempt to break free from the chains of the past and embrace the future forged from the lessons learned in the fires of our history.

With a heart that is slowly healing,
Your Adult Child,
Chris

Part Two - Adulthood

{ 4 }

Chapter Four

E ighteen to Twenty-One Years: The Search for Myself

I stepped into my newfound freedom, a world awash with possibilities, for I was an adult now—18 and ready to embrace life on
my own terms. No longer tethered to the constraints of adolescence,
I could feel the intoxicating rush of independence coursing through
me. In a year, I would legally be able to stroll into a bar, a thing
not particularly scrutinized in Rhode Island in 1983—where my peers
and I often found ways to sip cold beers long before the clock struck
midnight. Transitioning into college felt like an exhilarating leap
into the unknown. My culinary journey began with a meat-cutting
class that stretched from 6 p.m. to 11 p.m., a strangely comforting
routine that sank me deeper   into the rhythm of culinary school life.

Culinary school was a medley of experiences, an unpredictable tapestry woven with the threads of night classes, early morning kitchen
duties, and an assortment of varied coursework. The eclectic nature
of my education meant one trimester I would be attending classes in
the evening, and the next would find me waking up at dawn to serve
breakfast in the cafeteria. But none of that mattered to me; I was driven by a singular mission—to graduate and move to New York City,
the very place where my mother had dreamed of making a life for
herself when she arrived from Sweden in 1959.

The next four years became a voyage of discovery, a time when I sought hope and my true identity amid the chaos of youth. I arrived at school in September with my long, permed hair, only to be greeted with ridicule from my classmates during our mandatory seated courses—English, Math, and Menu Planning. In those evening classes, I often arrived stoned, treating the lectures as a mundane inconvenience, while writing papers felt like mere busywork. It was in this atmosphere that I encountered a jock from Chicago, who relentlessly mocked me as I entered the classroom, quipping, "Look, it's Jesus Christ and he arrived stoned!" Each taunt stung—each laugh echoed with memories of my early struggles, forcing me to confront my insecurities.

Upon returning home for the Christmas break, I decided it was time for a drastic change. I cut my hair short for good and embraced a new look, growing a mustache that transformed my appearance. This new direction shielded me from the barbs of my peers. My roommates barely recognized me, with one playfully rebranding me as "Senator Nicolas Papadapas." This transformation turned out to be more than just skin deep; it felt like a fresh start, and I hoped it would earn me some much-needed respect, putting an end to the haggling from the peanut gallery of college mockers.

Despite my physical metamorphosis, romantic endeavors remained elusive during my initial year at school. It wasn't until my second year that I began to navigate the often-treacherous waters of relationships. Most girls at school seemed disinterested in me, yet I garnered plenty of companionship with my roommates—one hailing from Florida, another from Massachusetts, and a third from Virginia. These guys introduced me to an array of recreational substances, from continued pot smoking and relentless bong hits to the hallucinatory escapades of mescaline, magic mushrooms, and acid. I find myself marveling at our older roommate who somehow managed to drive us from Providence to Boston, utterly wasted on mescaline.

Luck smiled upon me during those college years when a fellow student in my culinary program alerted me to a weekend job opening he had in Manhattan. The opportunity was at a prestigious restaurant perched 39 floors above the bustling city, offering stunning views of Central Park—a slice of heaven that felt almost surreal. Thanks to a four-day school week, I could leave class on Thursdays, share gas money with my friend, and embark on a three-hour drive to the city. This job allowed me to work every weekend, immersing me in the vibrant culinary scene, which made the pain from my past fade into the background like distant thunder.

Each shift at that Manhattan restaurant felt invigorating. I was no longer plagued by my history; I was absorbed in a world of kitchen chaos and culinary creativity, reveling in the opportunity to learn and grow. Fortuitously, I lived with my aunt in Westchester for free, a comfortable refuge allowing me to travel by train into the city on Fridays and Saturdays. Armed with the magnetic energy of youth, I was filled with hope, excitement, and a palpable sense that my dreams were finally within reach. I hadn't even graduated yet, yet here I stood, on the brink of realizing the life I had always craved.

As summer arrived, I turned 19 while working at the restaurant. To celebrate, my coworkers and I ventured to a bar in the East Village on 7th Avenue one Friday night after our shift. It was there that an older woman caught my eye and, against my better judgment, my friends nudged me to approach her. The ensuing night took a path I hadn't anticipated; she took me back to her Brooklyn apartment, marking a significant, if foggy, milestone in my life—I lost my virginity. The night was wrapped in beer-fueled haze, and to this day, I struggle to recall if I enjoyed that experience or continued merely feeling terrified when I woke up. The harsh reality struck me: I had just spent the night with a single mother, her young child sleeping just down the hall. In that moment, I felt a rush of shame as I scrambled to thank her, escaping as fast as I could back to Westchester on the subway and train, ruminating on the implications of this "one-night stand." I wanted my first experience to possess meaning and tenderness, but instead, it surrendered itself to the chaos of young adulthood.

While navigating the aftermath of my fleeting encounter, I found a friend from work who lived in Queens and introduced me to my first genuine long-term girlfriend, Gina. Just two years my junior, Gina had recently turned 18, and I was nearly 20. Our weekends became your typical long-distance romance; I would travel down from school to visit her, and our conversations were filled with stolen moments, facilitated by payphone cards long before the advent of cell phones. She embodied the spirited essence of an Italian Catholic girl—an archetype akin to the one Billy Joel immortalized in "Only the Good Die Young."

In our relationship, the physical expressions of affection took precedence; we mostly kissed and shared intimate moments, which left me compelled to focus on her pleasure over my own. Looking back, it's evident that this urge to prioritize her needs stemmed from my childhood wounds—an unconscious drive to avoid abandonment at all costs. Despite the innocent joy I felt in having a girlfriend, the relationship was built on a fragile foundation. My desire for validation often eclipsed genuine satisfaction, leaving me to grapple with embedded feelings of inadequacy.

In December 1985, I graduated from culinary school and relocated to Queens, where I shared a modest apartment with a fun-loving older roommate who was moving upstate. Bart became a source of amusement in my life; our shared living situation came with incredibly affordable rent—just $150 a month, including expenses. During this time, I juggled several jobs that spanned Long Island, Queens, and Westchester. As my relationship with Gina drifted apart, we amicably transitioned into friendship.

It was while working at a Westchester County hotel that destiny intervened once more, introducing me to Kiara, my future life partner. She was a stunning 20-year-old who left me speechless whenever she sat across from me during our work breaks; I often felt a lump rising in my throat as her mere presence made me forget what I was supposed to say or do. The prospect of this beautiful girl showing any interest in me was both exhilarating and disorienting. Eventually mustering the courage I needed, I penned my feelings in a sweet Hallmark card, and on that path paved with tentative hopes, we began dating in December 1986.

Our time together there was electric, and we found adventure in our spontaneity, relishing late nights filled with laughter, shared dreams, and the thrill of young love. I eventually moved closer to Kiara in Westchester County, and once my new roommate expressed discomfort about her frequent stays, we moved in together, solidifying what had become an inseparable bond.

Sexually, my life felt vibrant and healthy. While I didn't identify as addicted to anything, Kiara and I enjoyed our fair share of parties, drinking, and occasionally indulging in cocaine. The merriment of our time together offered a reprieve from the darkness I had battled earlier in life. She introduced me to the joys of camping and other affordable recreational activities, creating a rich tapestry of experiences I found exhilarating.

We thrived in our first year together, ignited by youthful passion and dreams of a life unimpeded by the burdens of the past. But just as the light of our happiness began to feel certain, tragedy lurked, lurking just around the corner—a reminder that life has its own plans, often utterly beyond our control. Shortly after I turned twenty-one, the weight of reality pressed down harder than ever before, and we were forced to confront the fragility of our existence. The world spun on, oblivious to the tumult brewing beneath the surface of our seemingly idyllic life, and as we dove deeper into the unknown chapters that lay ahead, the search for myself would take unexpected turns, whisking me on a journey that demanded even more courage, clarity, and resilience.

A letter to my Dead Parent

Mother,

I find myself reflecting on the path my life has taken since I set out on my own—not just as a young adult but as a dreamer, just like you. It's been a tumultuous journey filled with both highs and lows, moments of joy and realizations that echo with your absence. I wish you could have been here to witness the man I've become, to celebrate the success that mirrors your own dreams of New York City.

When I first stepped into culinary school, a world of endless possibilities unfolded before me. I felt your spirit guiding me, encouraging me to embrace the very freedom you longed for when you made the brave journey from Sweden in 1959. Just as you envisioned a vibrant life amid the bustling streets and soaring skyscrapers, I found myself eagerly drawing closer to that dream, crafting a life in the heart of New York City—a place filled with culinary ambition, creativity, and the vibrant energy you so desired.

In those formative years, however, I grappled with the weight of my past, haunted by insecurities and fears that often felt insurmountable. My experience in college became a battleground, thrusting me into a world that left me feeling exposed and vulnerable. The ridicule and judgment I encountered were difficult to navigate, and at times, it felt as though the chaos would swallow me whole. But through it all, I held onto the essence of your dreams and the steadfast belief that I could rise above it, just as you had.

I fought through those fears—transforming traumas into resilience. I cut my hair, reinvented my image, and, slowly but surely, I transformed the barbs of my peers into stepping stones toward self-discovery. Along the way, as I learned to embrace love, connections, and the thrill of youth, it became clear that your spirit was alive in every risk I took. I wanted you to witness my struggles and triumphs, to witness my growth from a scared boy into a passionate man chasing his culinary dream.

Yet, amidst this personal evolution, I cannot help but feel the sting of your absence. I wish you were here to experience the joys of my successes—my accomplishments that echo your aspirations. Your life was cut short too soon, leaving shadows where light should be. It pains me to think you missed bearing witness to the journey we both dreamed of, the one that culminated in the vibrant life I'm crafting every day.

As I navigate the world, armed with your love and inspiration, I promise to honor your dreams and fulfill the legacy you left behind. I am conquering the kitchen and finding my voice, stitching my own dreams into the fabric of New York City—the very city you once yearned for. I will continue to push through, transforming my surroundings into a narrative of courage, creativity, and brightness, punctuated by the memory of you.

Thank you for the dreams you instilled in me. I carry you with me—always. I hope that wherever you are, you can see a glimpse of my world and feel pride in the man I am becoming. I know I wouldn't be here without your love and guidance, and your memory fuels the fire within me. I miss you deeply, and I'll never stop striving to make you proud.

With love, Your Adult Child,
Chris

Chapter Five

Twenty-One to Forty Years: The Seeds of Addiction

At twenty-one, I stood at the precipice of adulthood, worn yet triumphant—a survivor of childhood's harrowing trials. I had embarked on a quest for self-discovery, meticulously sculpting a new identity that flickered with promise, purpose, and hope. It was a rite of passage that began with the painful excavation of buried traumas, but ultimately blossomed into a life I could embrace.

With every passing day, the bitter memories of my youth—like my father squandering my final student loan check on personal indulgences instead of my education—began to fade into distant echoes. For the first time, I felt the warmth of genuine support and unconditional love wrapping around me. My grandmother, a beacon of resilience in our family, stepped in to cover my tuition, ensuring that I could finally don my cap and gown. In the shifting tides of my new life, Kiera entered with her unassuming grace, her family showering me with kindness in a manner I had scarcely believed possible.

Through the prism of Kiera's family dynamic, I witnessed a vibrant tapestry of joy, laughter, and unwavering support. They lent a helping hand whenever needed, orchestrating moments of genuine connection that had long eluded me. This dynamic was an alien world to me, far removed from memories of my own home, where shared meals rarely happened, and the air was thick with unspoken resentment.

Kiera and I found a home in a modest apartment in the picturesque enclave of lower Westchester County, New York. Though it consumed nearly every penny we earned, the space felt like a sanctuary—a refuge filled with laughter and friends who instilled a sense of belonging. I had ventured into the realm of corporate food service, trading the frenetic chaos of restaurant kitchens for a more predictable rhythm that offered weekends free—a glimpse of the normalcy I craved. I flourished as a Sous Chef and, emboldened by a sense of camaraderie, proposed to a fellow assistant that we co-manage the kitchen when our Executive Chef departed. To our astonished delight, we were given the chance to operate a kitchen that served over 3,500 employees.

At just twenty-two, I ascended to the role of Executive Chef—a position I had coveted since I first wielded a chef's knife. My dreams unfurled before me like a sunlit path, beckoning me forward. But just as the fog of uncertainty lifted, another darkness crept in, threatening to engulf us both.

Kiera was not just my partner; she was the youngest of five siblings, and her brother, Jay, loomed large in the familial landscape. At twenty-nine, he battled the silent demons of depression and drug addiction, the struggle often hidden behind his jovial smile. His charm—a slight frame, dark eyebrows, and a disarming grin—belied the turmoil within. An argument had bred a rift between him and Kiera before we even moved in together, leaving her heart aching and bewildered. It haunted our family gatherings, where Jay would engage with everyone but Kiera, his sister, rendering her invisible.

This was my first real glimpse into the complexities of familial love and strife, a stark contrast to my own upbringing. I had come from a world where shared meals seldom occurred, where conversations were stilted and devoid of intimacy. In Kiera's family, I was thrust into a whirlwind of laughter and banter, interspersed with lovingly delivered jabs—her father's exuberance often directed at me. It was in these moments that I began to uncover the weight of familial bonds and the richness of connection.

Then, one fateful Sunday in November, the comforting rhythms of our lives shattered when Kiera received a phone call from her sister. Jay was in critical condition at the hospital. Within minutes, we raced against time, desperation propelling us forward. But fate had dealt a cruel hand; by the time we arrived, the doctor delivered the unthinkable news: Jay had passed away.

The room filled with palpable agony, and I felt every ounce of their collective sorrow as though it were a physical entity pressing down upon me. Kiera's heart-wrenching cries echoed through the anguish, reverberating in my chest. Compassion surged, yet my own grief remained a shadow, inscrutable and unfelt. I had buried my mother, my grandfather, and my grandmother, but this was different—a visceral manifestation of love ripped apart and mourning that stretched into the very soul. Witnessing Kiera's raw grief illuminated a truth I had long denied: mourning is a testament to love, a natural and healthy response.

In the face of such monumental loss, I found myself retreating into the recesses of my own guarded heart. Rather than offering the support that Kiera so desperately needed, I withdrew, labeling myself as a mere outsider to her family's tragedy. Quietly, I returned to work, clocking in like a machine, while nights passed in silent contemplation. I became a phantom in her world, observing the grief-stricken planning of Jay's funeral from a distance, awash in feelings of inadequacy.

As days bled into weeks, Kiera's emotional landscape shifted drastically. Her grief, so potent and raw, coursed through our relationship in waves of anger and despair. The laughter we once shared gave way to furious clashes and tearful evenings, leaving me trapped in my own fear and uncertainty. I felt a chilling isolation returning, pulling me back into the protective shell I had lived in as a teenager.

One fateful weekend, the weight of my despair compelled me to speak up—to confront the shadows lurking in my heart. "I think I should move to California," I uttered, my voice trembling under the weight of my fear. Kiera's response was swift and filled with anguish. "Are you breaking up with me? My brother just died! What could possibly prompt this?"

Her pain pierced through me, and in that moment, I struggled against the tide of my own instincts. Sadness wrapped around me as I grappled with the urge to flee—taking the easy road, leaving the pain behind. "I need space... This fighting, all this drinking—it terrifies me."

Miraculously, those words forged a connection rather than sever it. With Kiera listening, we navigated the torrent of our emotions together, reminding each other that love is a journey filled with challenges—not an escape route.

In the kaleidoscope of grief, Jay's death had ignited a resolve in us. We committed to replacing old habits with a promise of sobriety. Our modest apartment turned into a sanctuary of renewal, and soon we decided to trade our cramped quarters for a more serene abode:

a cozy loft above a garage, nestled in the tranquil landscapes of Putnam County.

While Kiera pursued her master's degree, I stepped into my new role as Executive Chef for corporate food service in Stamford, CT. However, the excitement of my new position soon gave way to discontent as the corporate world revealed its darker underbelly—most notably, a narcissistic boss who exploited his authority while stealing from the company. I found myself fed up, and after one fateful decision to report him, I became the target of his wrath, navigating his thinly veiled hostility every day.

Kiera recognized my discontent and suggested I consider a different path, one outside the culinary realm. This was a pivotal moment, and while I harbored trepidation about relinquishing my passion, I followed her encouraging nudges to find a job as a data entry clerk for a Christian nonprofit organization. The move felt alienating; I uprooted a decade of culinary experience to dig into the monotonous world of negative-option book subscriptions.

I sat behind a terminal processing requests—a mundane existence, yet oddly freeing as I transitioned from the relentless bustle of kitchens to a space where I could quietly breathe. As my mind danced between inspiration and familiarity, I stumbled into the vibrant yet rigid world of religion that had once ensnared my teenage soul.

One fateful encounter would send shockwaves through my life. While visiting my old team from the food service, I ran into a familiar face—the security guard who for years exchanged amicable greetings with me. When I shared that I was now in a new job, his expression shifted, and he posed a question that hung heavily in the air: "Are you a Christian?"

I answered honestly, "Yes." And then came the fateful follow-up: "What about Kiera? Is she saved?" This innocent exchange unleashed a cascade of memories from my past—reminders of the well-intentioned fear that had once gripped me, tales of damnation that haunted my teenage years. Before I knew it, I was spiraling back into the fervor I thought I had escaped.

As I dove deeper into my new role, I found myself clutching a Bible during my commute, attending morning prayer sessions, and delving into a world imbued with religious fervor. Kiera stood by, incredulous yet steadfast, cautioning me against the fervent beliefs espoused by those who didn't truly know me.

Months unfurled in a haze of spiritual turmoil, and finally, a moment of clarity pierced through the fog. I recognized that I was spiraling—losing touch with the essence of who I was in light of the dogmas I had begun to adopt. With Kiera's encouragement, I sought therapy, opening myself to new dialogues and, eventually, the transformative power of Adult Children of Alcoholics (ACoA) meetings.

These gatherings became a lifeline, unearthing emotions I had suppressed too long. I encountered fellow travelers who shared similar traumas, bonding over our struggles with alcoholic parents. In this supportive environment, I discovered my own voice—the beauty in expressing vulnerability and the right to feel deeply, to reclaim my humanity.

While I navigated the rocky terrain of personal growth, my career took an unexpected yet welcoming turn. Amid the burgeoning tech boom, I transitioned from data entry to head of computer operations—a role that nourished my passion for learning and creativity.

My old fears of inadequacy transformed into curiosity, igniting a flame within me that propelled me forward.

Kiera and I forged a life in a quaint town in Fairfield County, abandoning our previous life for a small cottage that blossomed with laughter, love, and an assortment of pets—four dogs, two fish tanks, and a beloved bunny. It was a chaotic yet beautiful existence, filled with everyday moments that bound us tighter.

In 1994, we decided to take the plunge, exchanging vows at her sister's summer rental in the Hamptons. I channeled my culinary skills into creating a memorable feast for our thirty guests, a testament to our love that had weathered the storms of life. Eight years of unwavering commitment led us to this moment, a reminder that our foundation had been tested and fortified.

In the aftermath of our wedding, an exciting opportunity beckoned from the bustling streets of Boston—an invitation to join a prominent technology team. We packed our belongings, our dreams pulsating with potential, and embraced our new journey. Kiera completed her degree, fueled beneath the weight of ambition, while I stepped into the world of corporate finance, where my skills flourished. The rush of technological advancement invigorated me, yet amidst the excitement, shadows whispered from the corners of my mind.

It was during this period that a younger co-worker dazzled me with his proficiency in UNIX and programming. Inspired by his zest, I took a leap of faith, transitioning to a contract position that offered an enticing pay rate, allowing me to maximize my earning potential. As the threadwork of my career developed, so too did Kiera's sense of contentment, waiting for our first baby to arrive in 1998.

Just a week before our firstborn entered the world, I received an opportunity that appeared to come at just the right moment—a lucrative offer from a recruiter in New York City. It called for us to relocate, bringing us nearer to Kiera's family and their unconditional support.

Three weeks after welcoming our son, we made the move back to New York. I began working in a prestigious downtown financial institution, utilizing my UNIX skills to support sophisticated trading systems. The pay soared higher than anything I had earned before, allowing us to secure a stable life and raise our son in a nurturing environment.

Yet past shadows crept into our lives, revealing old ghosts that would rear their ugly heads as we navigated a new home. When we applied for a mortgage, my father's past misdeeds surfaced—a secretly forged credit card and a mountain of debt that had once tarnished my credit report. The bitterness of his failure, echoing through my life, now threatened to impact my family's future.

After years of distance, my father's dark legacy now loomed over us, rekindling raw emotions I had tried so valiantly to escape. With Kiera's unwavering support, we reached out to my estranged stepmother, Kate, requesting her help to rectify the mess left by my father. To my relief, she responded positively, clearing the debt and enabling us to move into our new home just shy of our son's first birthday.

Our new life in Connecticut was blossoming until an unforeseen trauma struck when Kiera became pregnant with our second child in 2002—amid the chaos that unfolded during the attacks on 9/11. I found myself in Midtown Manhattan that fateful day, an agonizing witness to a historical tragedy. I was engulfed in disbelief, distress, and confusion as the towers fell, sealing the world in despair.

For hours, we were trapped in the building, shielded from the horror unfolding outside. Heart pounding, I managed to escape in the afternoon, overwhelmed by the surrealism of the day's events. No journey home had ever felt so endless. When I finally reconnected with Kiera, our embrace held the weight of fear and uncertainty about bringing another life into a world that had abruptly shifted.

In the aftermath of 9/11, life resumed its frenetic pace, filled with tender moments and daily chaos. Each morning, I boarded trains that carried me into the heart of Manhattan, working tirelessly while the shadows of lingering trauma wove through me like an unseen thread. Every evening, I returned home, not just to my children, but to the mounting stress and unspoken fears that thrummed beneath the surface.

The house we had purchased began to reveal its flaws, morphing into another source of pressure. The relentless rain exposed leaks, and cumbersome responsibilities piled on top of my growing anxiety. Kiera and I planted seeds of renovation plans into motion, only to come up against the cold reality of our fluctuating finances.

As my contractor's pay fluctuated, so too did the fragility of our finances. I watched in horror as the high anxiety of my career coincided with mounting pressure at home—leaving us struggling financially in the wake of uncertainty. Missing the warmth of open communication, I leaned in the opposite direction, throwing money toward bills, and indulging in extravagance none of us could afford.

It wasn't long before Kiera began to feel the chasm that had formed between us—a distrust laced with the pain of secrecy. To my astonishment, where I saw progress, she saw betrayal. The weight of miscommunication cracked the veneer of our love, and her trust in me shattered; a painful reminder that the past was not without scars.

The myriad of burdens began weaving an intricate tapestry of pressure, work anxiety, and the chilling onset of technology's incursion into our lives—smartphones beckoning and amplifying vulnerability. It was at this juncture, along the precipice of my demons, that the seeds of my deeply guarded addiction began to sprout.

Thrust into the escalating storm, I began to face the truths I had long buried. As the tumult of everyday life escalated, I unwittingly cultivated the very addiction I had sworn to escape—one that would lay siege to my existence over the next 15 years. The fragility of love, the weight of trauma, and the urgency of desperation began to intertwine, morphing into a tangled web I now found impossible to unravel. My seeds of addiction had been sown, laying dormant for decades and would reveal themselves in the next fifteen years where the trauma of life and financial stress would accelerate.

A letter to my Dead Parents

Mother and Father,

As I sit down to write this letter, my heart is heavy with the weight of all the words left unspoken, the moments that passed without you, and the love I've struggled to reconcile in your absence. A part of me longs for the comfort of sharing my journey with you, to let you know who I am today—everything I have become, and everything I have learned through both joy and suffering.

Life has been a tapestry woven with vibrant colors and painful threads alike. After you left this world, I found myself in a battle against the shadows of our past—shadows that conditioned me to walk through life guarded and afraid. But I want you to know that I fought those battles fiercely. I dug deep to unearth the forgotten smiles and laughter, the warmth of family, and the understanding that our upbringing didn't have to dictate my future.

In my early twenties, I began to mold my identity—to embrace the lessons I had buried so I could truly live. I found love in Kiera—an unconditional love that cradled the broken pieces of my heart. She stood by me as we crafted a life steeped in connection, where laughter filled our home, and resilience etched its way into our family's foundation. I wish you could have seen the joy in our children's eyes and the warmth that enveloped us during those family meals—each bite a testament to the love that grew from the ashes of pain.

However, the weight of loss still loomed heavy as I navigated through personal struggles, notably confronting my own addiction—a specter that threatened to derail all that I had worked for. In the rawness of recovery, I discovered a new strength within myself, piecing together the fragments of my past while allowing vulnerability to guide me toward healing. Kiera and I weathered storms together, finding solace in shared moments of honesty and openness, acknowledging the layers of our experiences and the ghosts that lingered.

I know you would have wanted to be there to see us—how we grew, how we laughed, and how we nurtured love over fear. I often wished to share with you the journey toward finding my passions anew, grounding myself in cooking and creating community. It gave birth to a culinary path that intertwined nourishment with connection—a practice that became a powerful extension of love to those I serve.

I want you to know that, despite the pain of your absence, your memories linger like a warm embrace. The lessons I carry from both of you have shaped my journey, illuminating the importance of love, trust, and perseverance. I've created my own family and forged bonds that echo with both the joy of laughter and the depth of shared sorrow.

If there's one thing I wish you could have witnessed, it is the strength and resilience I've built in your absence. I has taken time, but I've learned to embrace my past while forging ahead with hope—often drawn back to the essence of our interactions, feeling both the weight and the lifting of my spirit.

I honor you with the life I lead—a life defined not simply by the loss we shared but by the love I have nurtured within the walls I've built. I am grateful for the moments I still treasure, for the lessons you pass on in unspoken ways, and for the love I weave into the fabric of my family.

Know this: while I faced the darkness, I emerged not just as a survivor, but as a man who knows the true power of love and growth. I carry your legacy forward, hoping you follow along in spirit, shining with pride for the journey and growth I continue to strive for.

With Sadness, your Adult Son,
Chris

{ 6 }

Chapter Six

Forty to Fifty-Five Years - The Addiction and my Denial

Some call these the years of mid-life crisis. Anything can be an excuse. I acted like a victim but continued to survive. So much happened so fast during this time.

Up to this point, I had never really dabbled in pornography, other than in the early days of dial-up modem internet connections, where downloading pictures from various ALT.BINARY groups was commonplace. Back then, in the mid-90s, the connections were so slow that I risked being caught. Kiera was not a fan of me looking at porn, but mostly because I was so secretive about it. If she wanted intimacy with me, I felt shame and acted like a holy person, never willing to engage in such treachery. I was in denial. Just like that 14-year-old who discovered porn, I was addicted; I just didn't know how bad it was, and the smartphone changed everything for me.

Smartphones provided fast connections, allowing me to have my device, to stay in the bathroom or in my hotel bedroom, watching any genre I chose. I typically drifted into the Lesbian world, which was a clear turn-on for me given the trauma of my childhood. I lived a secret life that spiraled deeper into darkness and denial as my life stresses increased.

During this time, I began to notice signs of sexual dysfunction, especially as my consumption of porn increased along with my masturbation habits. I engaged in this behavior so many times a day that it was no wonder I couldn't provide Kiera with the satisfaction she deserved. She struggled to understand what was happening; we left it to aging, but the reality was that my addiction and compulsive acting out prevented us from having a healthy sexual relationship.

Life was particularly challenging around this time. Our boys were four and eight in 2006, and we decided to continue our renovation plans. I was contracting for a large international bank, traveling to Europe for the first time. Work was good, and I was making a reasonable pay rate that kept us afloat, despite burning through the Home Equity Line of Credit over the previous couple of years.

We had a lot on our plates—our boys were active in Scouts, and Kiera and I took on roles as Scout leaders during these next fifteen years. Additionally, our aging parents needed our help. I even moved my father—now divorced three times—up to Connecticut from Florida, as he was unable to care for himself. I subsidized his costs to live in an assisted living facility.

Kiera and I wanted to renovate our home to fix various problems, while also expanding the project to build a single-floor in-law suite for her parents. I needed a stable full-time job to make this happen, so in 2007, I accepted an opportunity to work back in Midtown Manhattan for an investment bank, marking a departure from the ten years of consulting I had previously done. This was to help me survive the volatile market and secure consistent pay to take on a much larger mortgage once we sunk another $600,000 into our renovation that began in 2008.

Things seemed to be going as planned until late 2008, when I watched as the institution I worked for went illiquid and was taken over by another large institution. This happened right in the middle of our renovation, where we were living in half of the old home while they finished working inside the new modular frame that was joining it. We were fortunate—I got to keep my job, although I had to fight for my pay after the merger with the new bank and get creative in finding a better role once the dust from the financial crisis settled.

During this period, I was anxious and stressed, yet I would never admit it. Each day, I went into work as I had done for the past ten years. I would come home, fulfill my responsibilities, try to be a good father to my boys, travel for work, and show up for scouting events. Kiera spent her days with the boys and her parents, who lived with us now in their new space. We continued to navigate our daily lives.

Unbeknownst to Kiera, I became more and more addicted to porn. I would binge when I traveled for work, isolating myself in hotel rooms and digging into new, unhealthy genres that were exciting yet toxic—living out fantasies rooted in childhood trauma. I kept this all secret from Kiera and lied to her for decades about my sexual fantasies, failing to recognize that my childhood trauma had set me on this destructive path.

Our sexual relationship continued to falter over time. Sex became rare, and I always had an excuse. I felt immense shame for not being able to perform for her, leaving her frustrated. The more I acted out secretly, the more I denied my feelings. I made excuses, justifying my behavior by telling myself that it was how all guys lived when they got older. I was delusional, completely in denial about my downward spiral.

Despite not cheating on Kiera physically, my mental fantasies about sex and masturbation were incredibly damaging. Toxic thoughts and fantasies took residence in my mind. Some of them led me to entertain perverse ideas about family members, echoing lessons I learned from my mother. Dark thoughts about the young boy struggling to hold his boundaries resurfaced as I watched porn genres that acted out these very scenarios. Things I believed my healthy self would see as taboo became intoxicating as I told myself I was not harming anyone, and so it was okay to indulge.

In truth, I was harming Kiera, myself, and my family, but I refused to admit it. My cravings felt justified—I had an intense need for relief, and porn became my drug of choice. I felt like a crackhead needing my next fix and searched for opportunities to be alone so I could act out. I lost countless hours that could have been used to improve myself and the lives of those I loved, instead feeding this addiction, which only grew from 2005 to 2020.

I used my stress as an excuse to justify this lifestyle. Tragedies like 9/11, financial turmoil, the economic crisis, and the COVID-19 pandemic all placed heavy burdens on us. Yet instead of confronting these challenges, I turned to porn, numbing out my pain and shirking my responsibilities.

It's incredibly difficult for me to recognize the good things that occurred during these fifteen years. I was selfishly blinded by my addiction, and the overwhelming shame I felt prevents me from appreciating the positive moments. Much did happen that was good, and I must try to remember that, but I was unable to take accountability for my actions. These fifteen years wreaked havoc on my marriage, especially when my truth was finally revealed to Kiera at the end of 2019.

During this time, our boys completed high school, and one even started college. We took care of our dying parents and buried them. We provided support for family members and hosted holiday meals at our home. We renovated and built a house we loved, raising our children in a safe place with great schools.

My dreams had come true. I built a home near New York, worked in the City, and lived a life I thought was worthy of pride. But in reality, it all felt empty. I had never truly healed and could not enjoy life or find genuine happiness. I lived a lie. I refused help and followed a path similar to my father—one of selfishness and fear.

These are the key topics I will address referencing my next five years of life, where I continued to harm Kiera, even through starting my recovery. Ultimately, however, I was finally able to reach a place of honesty with myself and her, allowing the healing to finally begin.

A letter to my Dead Parents

Mother, Father,

As I sit down to write this letter, I feel an overwhelming mix of emotions—grief, regret, and a lingering desire for understanding. I have spent many years navigating a tumultuous journey that originated in my childhood, shaped significantly by your choices and struggles. It's time you know how your lives, especially your battles with addiction, influenced my own path.

Looking back, I can see how the shadows of your addictions loomed over my formative years. The confrontation of alcohol and unhealthy relationships created an environment filled with confusion and turmoil. I grew up witnessing the chaos and pain that followed you both, and although I may not have understood it fully then, those experiences left an indelible mark on my psyche.

Becoming an adult, I thought I could escape the patterns of addiction that ensnared your lives, but I found myself trapped in my own set of destructive behaviors. In the years of my life when I should have been building a healthy family and nurturing genuine relationships, I spiraled deeper into my own addiction—this time fueled by pornography. Just as I had witnessed you both seek solace in your vices, I gravitated toward something that felt like relief but only exacerbated my shame and secrecy.

The addictions I faced were born from not just a longing for escape, but also a misguided attempt to numb the pain of unresolved trauma. The lessons I absorbed from you—the avoidance of honesty, emotional connection, and the tendency to seek comfort in unhealthy habits—played a significant role in my denial and ultimately my destructive choices. I often felt like a mere reflection of your struggles, perpetuating the cycle rather than breaking free from it.

I want you to know that I have reached a crucial point where I have begun to acknowledge these correlations. The revelations I uncovered within myself about my struggles have been profound. Just as your battles with alcohol and promiscuity impacted our lives, I recognize how my own addiction has harmed my family, particularly Kiera and our boys. I carried the weight of not just my demons but those I inherited from you.

Despite the love and lessons you offered in your own way, the darkness of addiction created barriers between us. Now, as I reflect on this chapter of my life, I realize I must embrace personal accountability. I cannot change the past, but I can work toward healing and understanding the patterns that have plagued our family for generations.

As I strive to mend my relationships and find healthier ways to cope, I want to honor your lives while also recognizing the lessons learned through hardship. I hope you can see that your struggles shaped my realities, and I am committed to breaking this cycle for my family. It's difficult, but I am dedicated to healing, to being a better father and partner, and to finally confronting the ghosts of our past.

Thank you for the life you gave me, flawed as it may have been. I carry the pieces of you with me, and I'm learning to build something new. May we find peace in this acknowledgment, and may my journey to recovery serve as both a tribute to your memory and a step toward liberation for generations to come.

Your Adult Son,
Chris

Part Three – My Recovery Journey

{ 7 }

Chapter Seven

A dmitting My Addiction

It was a typically cold day in early December 2019, a stark contrast to the warmth of the upheaval brewing inside me. I had recently been laid off from my job, but I was fortunate to quickly secure a new role at another bank, thanks in large part to a glowing reference from my former boss. The catch? This new position required me to relocate to Arizona.

I hadn't truly planned to come clean to Kiera about the depth of my addiction. In my mind, I figured she had some inkling that I watched porn, but she never confronted me directly about it. Her quiet observations of my behavior were often sharper than my own self-awareness. What I saw as my escapism, she saw as my attempt to run away—a truth I could not disguise from her piercing gaze.

As we discussed ongoing concerns and anxieties that weighed heavily on her, particularly surrounding my sexual dysfunction, I let something slip. In a moment of frustration, I uttered words that could cut through even the thickest fabric of our relationship: I implied that I wasn't attracted to her anymore. It was a devastating statement, one that I didn't truly mean but felt like an easy out. I was desperate for a release, a way to navigate around the confrontation that I so deeply feared.

Then, in a moment of raw vulnerability, I confessed my addiction. "I'm a porn addict," I admitted. The revelation hung between us, thick with the ramifications it carried. Kiera's eyes flickered with disbelief as she processed my words. The gears in her mind began to turn as she calculated the timeline of my addiction, connecting the dots to my impotence—not just physically but emotionally and relationally.

For years, she had wrestled with the nagging worry that something was fundamentally wrong with her, believing her worth was tied to my attraction to her. In truth, my dysfunction had roots far deeper than any of her perceived shortcomings. I had been seeking an escape route, all while meticulously constructing a facade to protect my inner turmoil.

Though still burdened with love for me, Kiera was faced with unimaginable choices. She could have fought to stay on the East Coast, clinging to the life we'd built, but instead she was considering packing up everything to join me in the West. I could sense that part of her longed for stability in the familiar, yet I selfishly thought only of the potential for relief that the move could bring us. Our house had become a money pit, a constant source of anxiety each winter as storms battered our home. I envisioned a life out West, with warm weather and a pool, mulling over how it could alleviate the rat race I felt stuck in, commuting daily to New York City.

In hindsight, moving out West may not have been a bad decision—especially when COVID-19 struck and turned the East Coast into a landscape of chaos and uncertainty. But that moment of decision-making was clouded by my entitlement, believing I deserved this new start while disregarding the emotional fallout it would inflict.

Coming clean about my addiction felt like a mere step in the right direction, but what followed was a three-year journey of continued suffering as I grappled with honesty and the deep-seated pain I was inflicting on Kiera. We packed our Connecticut home, placed it on the market, and experienced the whirlwind of selling it in just two weeks during the early summer of the pandemic. The city we once knew had come to a standstill, and we were exhilarated to break free from it.

The anxiety of bringing our older son home from college in Chicago and watching our younger son complete his senior year remotely felt overwhelming, reminiscent of the turmoil during the financial crisis of 2008. In January, I began remote therapy with a therapist I found back in Connecticut. It was a fresh start, and though my focus was on quitting porn, I realized I had a long way to go.

I wanted to be committed, but truthfully, I wasn't ready to give it up. I managed to cut back significantly, convincing myself I was serious about my recovery. Yet, I wasn't participating in any structured program that could genuinely guide me toward sobriety. As we settled into our new life, I found myself at a crossroads. The less I utilized porn, the more I turned to Kiera, but not in the loving, intimate way she deserved—instead, I objectified her to fulfill my cravings.

So much lay ahead of me, and I understood now I hadn't yet begun the true work of healing. I had a long journey to navigate, and it was clear I needed to face the intertwined truths of my addiction, my past, and the profound impact they were having on the people I loved the most.

Chapter Eight

My Recovery Begins

My journey toward recovery truly began when I stepped into the rooms of Sex Addicts Anonymous (SAA). The backdrop of COVID-19 complicated this path, as in-person meetings were suspended until the spring of 2021. My experience mirrored my time in Adult Children of Alcoholics (ACoA); I showed up, I talked, but I never engaged deeply with the program or embraced the steps with a sponsor.

For about a year, I drifted through SAA, attending meetings but continuing to relapse. Even during periods when I wasn't consuming porn, I found myself acting out in harmful ways, including being verbally abusive to Kiera. She didn't deserve the mistreatment I inflicted upon her, and in hindsight, perhaps separation would have spared her from my painful cycle of abuse. Unfortunately, she had no safe place to go, and we were both reluctant to waste resources on separation at that point in our relationship.

Over those five years, Kiera and I invested significantly in therapy. I tried EMDR—eye movement desensitization and reprocessing, a therapy aimed at helping with Post-Traumatic Stress Disorder. While it offered some relief, it didn't fully address the core issues that fueled my dishonesty with myself. It became evident that true healing would require more than individual therapy; it required a deep commitment to change at a fundamental level.

Amid this turmoil, Kiera embarked on her own recovery journey, finding the best therapist she ever encountered during this transformative process. One advantage of moving to Arizona was access to quality therapists and the opportunity to prioritize self-care. She discovered a renewed sense of agency, recognizing that her well-being was just as critical as my own.

I sought out various therapists, many of whom were certified in treating sexual addiction (CSAT), and participated in support groups, including one for men who had experienced sexual abuse. These experiences were vital, yet the real turning point came with my commitment to the 12-step fellowship of SAA.

In June 2022, I hit a crucial milestone: my last relapse. I took the bold step of getting a sponsor in the program. Over the next two years, I committed myself to working through the 12 steps with renewed diligence, achieving sobriety for the first time. I immersed myself in the literature, reading over 100 books on addiction and understanding its various manifestations in our lives. I started to see my addiction for what it truly was—a symptom of deeper pain, rather than the root cause itself.

Kiera and I also attended couples counseling with several therapists, all CSAT certified and specializing in sex therapy. This journey of healing our relationship incurred a substantial financial burden, as many of the skilled therapists we sought were not covered by insurance. But we knew this was an investment not just in our marriage, but in ourselves as individuals.

SAA offered invaluable support throughout my recovery. I attended 120 meetings in 120 days, often going twice in a single day. Daily check-ins with my sponsor and fellow members became my lifeline. I engaged with the program's materials, worked on my step assignments, and bravely shared my step story, offering a raw glimpse into my struggles and the meaning of recovery to me. These meetings provided a sense of accountability that had previously been missing from my life.

Despite these efforts, I recognized the necessity of additional therapeutic interventions, particularly intensive programs. My first intensive took place at The Meadows in Arizona, focusing on survivors of childhood trauma. That week proved transformative, enabling me to delve deeply into my pain and reconnect with the parts of myself I had long abandoned. The writings and videos of John Bradshaw, which I encountered through my ACA participation, also left a profound impact on my understanding of my past.

The most significant breakthrough occurred six months later when a therapist recommended the PCS program in Scottsdale, a renowned intensive treatment that promised life-changing results. It was, indeed, transformative for me. Despite the $10,000 cost, the investment was invaluable. I accessed emotions I never thought I could confront, and a crucial part of my recovery involved facing the demons that had held me captive.

Working alongside highly skilled therapists employing diverse modalities—EMDR, Psychodrama, Cognitive Behavioral Therapy (CBT), Dialectical Behavior Therapy (DBT), and others—greatly enriched my recovery experience. These approaches helped me reprocess the pain I had long suppressed, offering me a new way to navigate my emotions instead of defaulting to destructive behaviors.

During this time, I also acknowledged my anxiety disorder, which led me to a psychiatrist who prescribed Celexa. This medication significantly enhanced my distress tolerance and reduced my compulsive urges to act out, both sexually and otherwise. It was not a magic bullet, but it provided me with the stability I needed to do the deep work required for lasting change.

As I reflect on this journey from 2020 to 2024, I see it as more than just a process of achieving sobriety—it was a complete redefinition of my existence. For so long, I had believed that I was broken beyond repair, that my shame and compulsions would forever dictate the course of my life. But through therapy, fellowship, and relentless self-exploration, I discovered that healing was possible.

Recovery has given me something I never thought I would experience: a sense of inner peace. I no longer live in constant fear of my own impulses, nor do I carry the unbearable weight of secrecy and self-loathing. The guilt that once consumed me has been replaced by a deep commitment to honesty, integrity, and self-respect.

This journey has also redefined my relationship with Kiera. While the wounds of betrayal do not heal overnight, our commitment to transparency and growth has fostered a deeper connection than I ever thought possible. We continue to walk this path together, not as a perfect couple, but as two individuals choosing every day to love and support one another.

To anyone struggling with addiction, I want to offer this message: you are not alone. No matter how lost you feel, no matter how impossible change seems, there is a way forward. Recovery is not about achieving perfection; it is about choosing, moment by moment, to move toward healing.

There is no quick fix, no easy way out. It requires effort, vulnerability, and the willingness to confront truths that may be painful. But if you stay the course, if you do the work, you will discover a life that is richer, more fulfilling, and more meaningful than anything addiction could ever offer.

I am living proof that even the most broken among us can heal. The road ahead is long, but it is also beautiful. And if you take that first step, you just might find that the best version of yourself has been waiting for you all along.

{ 9 }

Chapter Nine

M**y Addiction to Lying**

In the years that followed my initial disclosure, I came to understand something about recovery that I hadn't anticipated: stopping the addictive behaviors was just the beginning. During those first years after sitting across from my wife and finally admitting the secrets I had kept buried for so long, I believed that progress meant simply abstaining from acting out. I thought sobriety was the finish line, the thing that would magically repair the damage I had inflicted on my marriage and my life. But I was painfully wrong. Abstinence from the behaviors that defined my addiction wasn't enough. Sobriety as a concept did nothing to address the years of lying, gas-lighting, and emotional abuse that had become second nature in my relationship. And it definitely didn't begin to touch the deep well of shame I had buried within myself.

In hindsight, the first four or five years after that initial confession were some of the most painful years of my marriage, and I was the reason why. I had disclosed a small portion of my truth—the fact of my sexual addiction—but I was far from ready to embrace honesty as a way of life. Disclosure was supposed to be a fresh start, yet I used it as a tool to further manipulate my wife and avoid doing the deeper work that recovery required of me. I convinced myself that saying the words "I'm a sex addict" was enough to call myself honest, even as I continued to hide my emotions, suppress my vulnerabilities, and hold back critical details about the damage I had caused.

Deep down, I was still lying—not just to her but to myself, too. I was claiming I was on the path to healing, but the truth was, I wasn't willing to confront the toxic shame that had lived inside me for decades. That shame had been the driver of my behaviors, the shadow that pushed me into addiction, and the voice that told me I was broken and unworthy of love. It was easier to focus on my outward sobriety than to admit to myself the extent of the harm I had caused or to face the parts of me I was most terrified to confront. My dishonesty continued, and my wife paid the price.

Instead of meeting her pain and fear with compassion, I gaslit her. When she tried to express what she was feeling— the anger, hurt, and betrayal—my first instinct wasn't to validate her experience or listen in any meaningful way, but rather to defend myself. I painted myself as the victim, turning the conversations back on her in ways that left her questioning her own reality. I minimized her pain, trivialized her triggers, and dismissed her fears. I rationalized and justified these actions to myself, telling myself that I was doing enough simply by not acting out sexually.

But the truth is, I was still harming her, just in subtler ways. My lack of honesty, my defensiveness, and my inability to own my emotions perpetuated a cycle of abuse. I manipulated her into believing I was making progress in my recovery while continuing to betray her trust on a deeper emotional level. I wasn't cheating on her anymore, but I was still making her feel unseen, unheard, and unsafe. It's a strange and heartbreaking thing to understand now: even as I walked the outward path of sobriety, the very tools of my addiction—secrecy, deflection, and gas-lighting— were alive and well in my marriage.

I avoided taking accountability for so much because I didn't want to shine a light on the things I hated most about myself. I still hadn't accepted that my lying and defensiveness weren't just residual habits—they were addictions in their own right. I fed those addictions every time I turned away from my wife's pain, every time I withheld my feelings, and every time I told myself I was doing better while avoiding the hard truths.

The turning point didn't come quickly or in a single moment; it came slowly, painfully, and in pieces. My wife started to pull back emotionally, weary from trying to make sense of the mixed signals I was giving her. She was triggered often, and rightfully so. For so long, I thought recovery for me was just about rebuilding myself, but what I hadn't recognized was that recovery, in the context of a relationship I had fundamentally broken, requires continuous work from both partners. For her, the effort meant finding enough strength to confront the heartbreak I had caused and decide if I was even worth staying with. For me, it meant showing up for that heartbreak with relentless honesty, no matter how hard it was, no matter how much shame became exposed.

The hardest but most important work in recovery is facing yourself and your darkest truths, but I didn't do this early on. I resisted putting myself fully into therapy. I skimmed the surface, claiming to make progress but avoiding the very things that were keeping me stuck: my guilt, my shame, and my anger. Shame, in particular, was my anchor. It fueled my desperation to escape vulnerability, to avoid the deep trauma I carried from my childhood, and to cling tightly to a narrative where I was still in control. But shame is insidious. It doesn't disappear just because you intellectualize your behaviors or stop acting out. Shame lives in secrecy, and to get rid of it, you have to bring it into the light.

For years, I refused to do that work, and it cost my wife dearly. When I wasn't gas-lighting her, I was invalidating her reality by shutting myself down emotionally. I couldn't show up with authenticity and vulnerability because those things required an honesty with myself that I hadn't achieved yet. Instead, I continued to hold back pieces of myself, just as I always had. Outwardly, I was gaining sobriety from my worst behaviors, but inwardly, I was still clinging to dishonesty because I wasn't ready to confront the full scope of my pain—or hers.

Thinking about those years is difficult because I know I caused so much additional harm during a time that should have been about healing. My wife, who had already endured decades of betrayal and deceit, had to sit with the harsh reality that the man standing in front of her, claiming recovery, was still lying—sometimes in words and sometimes by omission. My inability to be honest kept us in a state of prolonged chaos, where neither of us could heal because the wounds were still being poked and prodded, never given the space to breathe.

Eventually, things began to change, but not because of some miraculous moment of clarity. They changed because I started to understand that recovery isn't something you sprint through or finish. Recovery is a lifelong commitment to being rigorously honest with yourself and others, every Letters to my Dead Parents single day. It requires a willingness to sit in discomfort, to face the fear and shame that inevitably arises, and to speak your truth no matter how vulnerable or terrifying it feels.

One of the hardest lessons I've learned is that healing doesn't erase the pain—for either partner. The pain lingers, the scars remain, and triggers still show up in unexpected ways. When they do, the question becomes: How will I meet that pain? Will I shut it down like I used to? Will I deflect, gaslight, or lie to minimize its impact? Or will I find the strength to stand in that discomfort, to acknowledge it, and to use it as an opportunity to deepen honesty and connection?

The work never stops in a relationship that has been harmed through this kind of abuse. Even now, years later, there are moments when I feel fear creep up, moments when my brain tells me it might be easier to shrink back into dishonesty. Those moments don't disappear completely, but what's changed is my commitment: I don't act on those thoughts. I don't let my fear dictate my response to the people I love. I've learned that fear is a part of being honest—it never really goes away. The difference now is my capacity to deal with it in the open, with courage, humility, and transparency.

Today, I continue to work diligently on myself, not just for my own recovery but for the well-being of my relationship. I've committed fully to therapy, to programs like SAA and ACA, and to the daily practices that keep me grounded. My shame no longer controls me, though there are still moments I have to actively remind myself of the tools I've gained. I've learned how crucial it is to constantly check in with myself, to be aware of when dishonesty—even in its smallest forms—threatens to return, and to stop it at the root.

I used to think that healing my marriage meant going back to what it was before my addictions came to light, but I now know that's impossible—and that's okay. The goal of recovery isn't to return to what was; it's to rebuild something new, to create a relationship built on a foundation of truth and vulnerability. That foundation wasn't there before, but we're building it now, brick by brick, every time I have the strength to show up honestly, even when it hurts.

Sobriety is not the same as recovery. Recovery is about more than abstinence—it's about how I live, how I love, and how I face the hardest parts of myself. To truly heal a damaged relationship, the work can never stop. It requires relentless honesty, rigorous self-awareness, and the courage to meet pain when it comes, instead of running from it. I've learned this the hard way, but I'm grateful to finally be on a path where I'm living it every day. For the sake of my wife, for my marriage, and for myself, I'll keep doing this work—for as long as it takes

{ **10** }

Chapter Ten

M y Sobriety

Sobriety has become much more than simply abstaining from harmful behaviors; it embodies a profound shift in my state of mind—a transformation rooted in contentment, honesty, and peace, both with myself and with those around me. It is not just a matter of avoiding addiction; it's about creating a life that no longer relies on the crutch of those compulsive behaviors. Sobriety is not deprivation; it is liberation—a fierce reclamation of my identity.

In the early stages of my recovery, the struggle to abstain felt overwhelming. My mind screamed for the comfort of familiar habits, the numbing distractions that had kept me sheltered from my pain for so long. Resisting those urges was far more than a test of willpower; it necessitated uncovering the deeply buried wounds that fueled my compulsions. I learned that stopping the behavior was merely a first step. True sobriety demanded the excavation of the self, an unyielding journey into the heart of my suffering and self-deception.

Sexual addiction is one of the most insidious afflictions to confront. Unlike substances that can be entirely abandoned, sexuality is woven into the very fabric of our existence. It is essential for connection, intimacy, and identity. But my relationship with sex had become distorted, tainted by a past that morphed something inherently beautiful into a compulsion steeped in secrecy and self-destruction. What should have been a source of connection devolved into a means of isolation.

For decades, I bore the weight of a double life. I constructed walls of deceit, convincing myself that as long as I could shield my darkest impulses from view, they did not exist. But secrets are relentless; they grow like tumors, infecting every crevice of one's existence. The burden of deception seeped beyond my own soul, poisoning my marriage, friendships, and sense of self. Kiera, my beloved wife, unknowingly bore the brunt of my addiction long before she even knew the depth of my struggle. She suffered from the consequences of my absence, my disconnection, my inability to authentically love her while I was drowning in my shame.

When my addiction was finally revealed, it erupted like a volcano, shaking the very foundation of our marriage. For Kiera, it felt like betrayal in its rawest form. How could she trust the man who had interwoven lies into the fabric of our life? How could she envision a future with someone who had hidden so much? These haunting questions lingered as I stood at a crossroads: either I could lose everything or commit to change.

In the rooms of SAA, I encountered stories that mirrored my own, where each confession resonated painfully with my own sins. Yet within those spaces, I discovered hope. I witnessed men and women who had crawled through the depths of despair, emerging into the light of accountability and redemption. Their experiences became beacons of possibility, illuminating the truth that transformation was achievable, that healing was no longer an abstract concept but a tangible reality.

Today, my sobriety stands as a testament to living a life infused with hope—a life dedicated to repairing what was once broken, rebuilding trust piece by piece, and making amends not just through words but through my daily actions. Sobriety involves showing up, being present, and choosing love over fear, honesty over comfort, integrity over expediency.

I share my story through this book because I understand what it feels like to be trapped within the suffocating grip of addiction, to feel that change is unattainable, that the damage done is beyond repair. I've grappled with the feeling of being a monster, both in perceiving myself through the distorted lens of shame and believing that I was undeserving of redemption. But I also know this: recovery is possible. Healing is real. The person you were in your darkest moments need not remain your permanent identity.

My sobriety has granted me more than just clarity; it has instilled in me a sense of purpose. It has taught me that true freedom is not found in indulging every urge but mastering them. I have learned that I am not defined by my past, that my mistakes do not dictate my worth. Each day, I focus on reconciling the harm I've caused and strive to be the man Kiera deserves, the father my children can admire, and the friend who stands true. This commitment to integrity and love is the legacy I want to leave behind.

To those who find themselves struggling, standing at the same precipice I once faced, remember this: you are not alone. You are not beyond redemption. The road ahead is fraught with challenges; there will be days when you stumble and question whether your efforts are worth it. Yet, I promise you this—if you dedicate yourself to healing, if you embrace the process of recovery, if you grant yourself the grace to move forward, you will discover a life far richer than what addiction ever promised.

Sobriety is not merely about abstaining; it's about what you cultivate in its place—how you rebuild relationships, embrace the truth, and step into the light. It's about the realization that, despite the wreckage, you are still worthy of love, peace, and happiness.

This is the truth I wish to impart dear reader. You are capable of change. You deserve healing. And no matter how far you have fallen, there is always a path back to the light. Each of us are resilient and each carries the potential for transformation within ourselves; it is time to embrace that truth and embark on your own journey. As I conclude this book, I carry forward the hope that echoes in my heart—that healing and love are always within reach, waiting for you to embrace.

Resources

Recovery Books recommended by Chris J. Murphy

There are nearly 100 books I have read during my five years of recovery, all of which significantly helped me face myself and learn to be honest with myself. Below is a collection of my top influential books that I recommend which you may also find helpful in your own healing journey.

The Murray Method - by Marylin Murray
Out of the Shadows - by Patrick Carnes
The Betrayal Bond - by Patrick Carnes
Broken Toys, Broken Dreams - by Terry Kellogg
Facing Codependency - by Pia Melody
I don't want to talk about it - by Terrence Real
Complex PTSD - by Pete Walker
No Bad Parts - by Richard C. Schwartz
Lonely all the time - by Dr. Ralph Earle
Healing the Shame that binds you - by John Bradshaw
Homecoming - by John Bradshaw
Family Secrets - by John Bradshaw

Treatments Chris J. Murphy experienced that he recommends helpful in Recovery to those who have similar stories.

PCS - Psychological Counseling Services - Scottsdale AZ. : A one week intensive treatment that provides extensive therapies with many different therapists including individual and group sessions.

The Meadows - Survivors 1, Wickenburg, AZ : A one week intensive focused helping individuals work through their childhood trauma events that occurred from ages birth to 18

12 Step Groups - These include Adult Children of Alcoholics (ACA), Alcoholics Anonymous (AA) and Sex Addicts Anonymous (SAA). These were highly valuable in my recovery with accountability and sharing my story that was necessary to heal and grow. 12 Step Groups are also cost effective compared to therapy sessions and can also augment the recovery process

Group Therapy - I joined a weekly male sexual abuse survivors group for over year and this had a huge positive impact on my recovery when listening and sharing deep painful stories and secrets with other survivors

Individual Therapy - I did many hours of therapy over these five years including various modalities such as DBT, CBT, EMDR, Accelerated Resolution Therapy (ART) and Emotional Transformation Therapy (ETT). All were very helpful for me to get in touch with those lost parts of myself that needed to be rescued and cared for.

Feel free to visit https://letterstomydeadparents.com to learn more about the book and find additional resources and blogs that may help in your recovery journey.

Letters To My Dead Parents

The DAILY WORD *for*

ANYBODY AND EVERYBODY

Inspiration Thoughts

CYNTHIA MARTA SMALL

CITI OF BOOKS

CITIOFBOOKS, INC.
3736 Eubank NE Suite A1
Albuquerque, NM 87111-3579
www.citiofbooks.com
Hotline: 1 (877) 389-2759
Fax: 1 (505) 930-7244

Ordering Information:

Quantity sales. Special discounts are available on quantity purchases by corporations, associations, and others. For details, contact the publisher at the address above.

Printed in the United States of America.

ISBN-13:   Softcover   979-8-89391-584-6
                  eBook   979-8-89391-586-0
                  Hardback   979-8-89391-585-3

Library of Congress Control Number: 2025905584